Manage Your Conversation

265 Inspirational Quotes

Motivational Quotes

and

Positive Quotes about Life

With these quotes you will always have an answer for your

questions

You will be able to manage your conversation very

well

S. Ramkhelawan

Introduction

Procrastination

The major reason why you may fail is procrastination.
Procrastination is the regular delaying of your duties and
activities for a long time. When you are procrastinating you
simply refuse to pick up a tool and start working. In such
case it does not matter how important the work is. You are
not concerned about the consequences that may follow
from further delaying your duty. Do not let this happen to
you.

(PHRASES)

Below I present a number of phrases, quotes to support

your conversation

265 Inspirational Quotes, Motivational Quotes

and

Positive Quotes about Conversation and Life

You can use them in single or combined.
Remember, confronting the other party with circumstances or facts can be very useful, but be careful with this; you should both come true.

1. Ask who-, what-, where-, when-, wh-y, and how questions.

Why questions are particularly suitable, they also have something philosophical. Philosophers are drilled and trained in asking the why question.

2. We should not deal with imperfections from the past, let's focus on the future.

3. You give only one side of the case. You should also do it from the other side.

4. If someone makes good comments to what you are saying, and you do not want to get involved, you can say: "That's a good starting point, I will think about it."

5. One can neutralize a reason for resistance, by exaggerating, by downplaying. One can negate the resistance by emphasizing own positive items.

6. Those arguments are far-fetched.

7. If someone launches a plan, analyze the total plan view with which points suits you, Those points one must be emphasized and the others just do not talk about it..

8. Sometimes use the rhetorical question and do not respond to challenges. A rhetorical question supposes, that the other party agrees to what the transmitter (speaker) suggests.

For example:

"Do you still care?"

"Do you still want to earn a lot of money later?"

9. Sometimes you can say on an offer/proposal:

Too late and too much.

Too late and too little.

Too early and too little.

Too early and too much.

Note

---

10. Is someone coming with a bad example, one can say. "This is an isolated case, an example of what should not be done. "and then emphasize the positive points of the majority.

11. I am assuming that everyone aids by the agreements.

12. I have said this to you and, you still are asking why?

"Because we might be too critical." "We must ask ourselves whether we can handle all of this."

13. The issue has left quite a bit of annoyance and disappointment.

14. During a conversation, Let see what you all did to make a positive impression. In order to strengthen that you can sometimes also mention the negative points of the other part. "I am of good will, that is my style of negotiation; I approach things from a positive attitude, that testifies my entire career."

15. If someone asks a question see if it is a question or a packaged convicted.

16. I can not change the agreement anymore but I still can make reservations.

17. Giving up privacy is the hardest thing there is.

18. My words are differently explained. My statements are taken out of context.

19. In a hard attack strike back hard or one can say: "I'm a little used to it. I can take away from there. "

20. At first there were some misunderstandings, there was perhaps talk of mutual incomprehension.

21. Sometimes you can say: "I'm going to take this or that step"and later perspective with: "that was a possibility."

22. In the case of threats, difficult negotiations, one breaks, stalling the other party. Think about a strategy.

23. Sometimes you can attack someone better with one word than wirh 10 ideas.

Note

_____

_____

_____

_____

_____

_____

24. It's better in difficult topics to be an entertaining person and avoid to make exact statements.

25. Traditionally, it is unsympathetic that the good suffer under some evils.

26. The most difficult problem to overcome is the problem that we do not see. If we do not see that something is a problem, we come not on the idea to do something about it.

27. The last time you were serious and uncertain. But you are definitely not on your friend.

28. Sometimes does someone have a disturbed relationship with the truth.

29. With each agreement; How do you check that the agreements also be complied with?

30. I have listened to your conversation with increasing amazement. I sincerely believe that there is a large, gaping misunderstanding

31. Do you know how he thinks? "Yes, but I am not going to tell you. "

32. I believe in your good intentions, but I'm afraid that.................

33. That is at least a little lucky situation.

34. Understanding is something else than to agree.

35. Why have you not mentioned this before? "Because we had underestimated the problem."

36. What will you do? "I don't know yet, I'm going to see what can not and what should not .

37. What has moved you to do that? It gives us problems. "It was a desperate act."

38. The individual ignorance is only partly to solve. Persons concerned must also take note of the information.

Note

_____

_____

_____

_____

_____

_____

39. If someone proposes something you don't agree with, you can say: "I wish you good luck with your intention."

40. In case of problems, lay everything out and say: "What can you do for me?"

41. I have acted in good faith on the information, that was given to me by the Secretariat.

42. I want a major satisfaction it is not about the money.

43. If you quote someone quotes, quote him the right wayand correctly.

44. By quoting select one can prove everything.

45. We do not live in the fear of the next attack round. But developing own opinions about task and future as much as possible ahead of time.

46. We need to work together and don't blame on each other. If we do not change the current situation there is no future for us.

47. It is not just a question of childishness or jealousy, but also a sense of insecurity.

48. I consider this to be a victory of the common sense.

49. The word trick does not belong to us, but in the circus.

50. That is an intorable question. I'm not a Crone walking behind everything jam.

51. If someone says: "you are here to answer the questions one can say: "But you have no right to silence me, I should tell my story too. "

52. It is only human that people forget or deny some things.

53. I could not get rid of my story.

Note

54. What are you doing?

How is it going?

Is it the truth?

Have we done everything we could?

Are there things we could not handle?

55. Sometimes a hard pronunciation is necessary to stop a discussion

56. I have no explanation for what happened.

57. About officials and aid workers. Do they do their job well or properly? Do they fit our laws on the right way?

58. If someone says: "I think this or that about you, or something with you to do " you can answer as follows: "So, you think that that is true?"

59. His decisions are completely the opposite in comparison with all previous insurances that he has done regarding this matter since...........

60. During a negotiation there is a tendency to overcharging.

61. Why do you talk about this and not about that? Answer: "because I can't talk about everything at once."

62. It is not about people, but about the policy conducted.

63. If someone first make good comments about you and afterwards attacks you, you can say:

"Are you confused?"

64. Sometimes there is reason to respond in a way that the other does not expect. Think of the journey of Anwar Sadat to Israel.

65. Regret speaking out is all too easy when it comes to words which anyone could have thought.

66. In provocative comments can you say: "I assume he has such tantalizing statements to stimulate the discussion. "

Note

---

67. What is it: "perjury or a difference of interpretation?"

68. Precisely because of the research he had understood that in good faith, errors were made.

69. Keep expectations of a discussion low, you can post easy say that the result is good.

70. It was an appointment with a responsible, for example, an official, who was competent to act so.

71. Sometimes one seizes external influences to cover internal failure.

72. Your attitude says a lot about the intentions you have regarding the decisions to be made.

73. I have no explanation for what has happened.

74. What is leadership?

That's to determine guidelines in the company and send it to the people, so they have clarity about what should and what should not. Leadership also means dealing with signals (feedback) from the staff/stakeholders regarding directives that you send.

75. You will when delivering criticism have to take intoconsideration some limits of the realities that also count for the opposing team, opposition.

76. We are satisfied with what has been achieved after lengthy discussions regarding the trip, the delegation, representation, etc.

77. If unexpected party is chosen.
"I didn't have asked that clarity, which is more or less provided to me. That clarifies the matter."

78. In dealing with people.
How to give them the idea that you appreciate them.
How do you pretend that they contribute, even though they sometimes have none.

79. As a consequence of the program delays and budget overruns, there is a liquidity problem. A strengthening of equity is therefore necessary. On how this should be done is currently under consultation.

Note

_____

_____

_____

_____

_____

_____

80. Sometimes you can, if you don't agree with the results of a thorough research challenge, the procedure or method of examination.

81. If not, clear who has done something, you can say: "I think so slowly that no one did it. But it is shown to have happened.

82. It is almost always true that he who pays, wants to determine what is happening with the money.

83. There is a misunderstanding, and there is indeed a communication disorder from which we get nervous.

84. In asking for help.
Ask or require help? "Would you please" sounds more attractive than, "I want you...................."

85. Sometimes someone is grasping ideas like a nanny. Has lack of creativity, thinking, laziness or lack of fantasy. It then seems like that his current level of knowledge is the highest possible.

86. Our work is unjustly discredited.

87. How shabby you will feel if you unjustly are seen for defaulter.

88. There should be these days a retroactive relief about that action in the past which everyone rejected .

89. You must give a true and fair view of the actual extent of the damage, the unrest, crime, etc.

90. A man is a community being. Please try to deal with others as you would like to be treated yourself.

91. You should always keep your own dignity.

Lose control of yourself?

That can't be right?

You become weak, you will be vulnerable

92. Good fences make good neighbors.

93. The task of the representative is to represent the people to monitor the Government, and together with the Government to make laws.

The problems are complicated single advocacy is not possible.

94. Sometimes, one needs to make decisions that do not correspond to the short term needs of the grassroots.

95. You have to make sure that the reporting, your statements, never conflict with the interests of your organization or your own.

96. Always think of

1. What do I do on my own accord?

2. What do I do in response to what the other person says or does?

97. As long as I am not giving you an answer, you can not even suspect what I am going to reply.

98. Better a living dog than a dead lion.

99. We will try to match your invitation as much as possible with our agenda.

Note

_____

_____

_____

_____

_____

_____

100. If people come here with closed minds, I have no damn chance to convince them?
It that case it becomes a nondiscussion.

101. It is always good to think. Thinking never harms.

102. According to the lawyer........ acted unlawfully by declaring that .... (fact)............... that has not taken place

103. It is good, pending a court case, negotiation, not to make comments.

104. That act is an unacceptable low point.

105. He uses a kind of salami tactics, with each time a piece of security, employment is broken down under the pretext of rationalization, effectiveness and automation.

106. In order to avoid misunderstandings, I wish to declare that with emphasis that stupidity and illiteracy are no synonyms, of which he is a living proof.

107. The law obliges the state its organs and officials to confidentiality about the ins and outs of the citizens and the data of the citizens. Officials/managers are held to secrecy.

108. The facts must be judged objectively by all parties, regardless the private or personal insights

109. I'll give you the opportunity to say: "the state of affairs was not good."

110. If there are apologies that should be offered, it's your turn then.

111. It's nice to hear how the arguments are adjusted.
It does not matter what arguments are put forward.
One picks them up just out from anywhere..

112. From a common friend I have learned that I can trust you.

113. He did not want to come, because the invitation was based on the wrong assumption.

Note

_____

_____

_____

_____

_____

_____

114. One of the outcomes was that the stakeholders, who were not satisfied with the product/service, had complained and had gotten any satisfaction, their criticism was ventilated to ten other people.

115. Every person is innocent until his guilt is proven

116. He left due to disagreement about the policy to be pursued.

117. The officials/aid workers should have a helpful attitude in their work regarding citizens and their interests.

118. Your work is making you paranoid, you are up to vacation.

119. Set out your track record without much emphasis. Set out achievements on a wide area and try to push the opponent on the defensive by emphasizing certain behavior now or in the past.

120. He tries to belittle the reporting by saying that there was nothing new in the State.

121. He saw that his words would have no effect.
After all, as had the experience learned, particular ideas
will not disappear, nor by reasonable arguments nor by
wise counsel.

122. In the fierce attack by the counterpart you can say:
"I can't help that the counterpart has collapsed.

123. The discussion is very concrete, clear in my view.
I don't let others provide me alibis by. They need to take
their own decisions.

124. Some reluctance had graced him, if only to avoid the
impression that he came to the same questionable level as
the others.

125. The judge makes decisions on the basis of evidence
that is legitimate and convincing. In their absence, there
must be acquitted.

126. My compliments for your sense of duty and
dedication.

Note

_____

_____

_____

_____

_____

_____

127. Do no try to convince someone sometimes, just let see what you would do in such a case.

128. However, you have failed adequately to address the human dimension.

129. A lack of inner civilization.

130. Is it true what he says?
So is it and this is how we do it.

131. In the case of a suspicion must be a reasonable suspicion

132. In the case of gossip I see it so differently: "to make it a bit bluntly, if I walk on the street, I know that there are sewers below. But I walk on the street. I don't sit in the sewers ".

133. We don't accuse you and work you not against you. This is our common analysis, which leads to our conclusion that this is best.

134. Suddenly, without any cause the man threatened me, us, the others under the outbreaks of abject curses.

135. In the post hearing of facts.
The fact that there was no openness make that we feel misled. If we had been informed about the facts and not heard by accident or trough others, we would say: "that's over forget it." But now there is a lack of confidence. We do not wat this kind of situations.

136. It occurs to me that you are accustomed to crass statements. That will no doubt have to do with your upbringing.

137. The best navigators are on shore.
"I'm not a navigator."

138. I agree with you, but I was step lower.

139. It is reasonable and fair for all parties contribute a proportional share of the proof or facts.

140. Sometimes the moral has the same size as the wallet.

Note

141. On the basis of my function I demand that.
"You can't reasonably demand that from me."

142. A visitor who is clearly less concerned.

143. An old proverb: "You can use dirty water to put fires out."

144. The aid worker must explain the patient in easy-to-understand language, the disease, prognosis, the treatment method, and the possible side effects. The right of the patient/client should be respected; He is free to decide on the treatment method.

145. Target of false accusations, blatant lies, and false representation of conviction.

146. Who wants to be everyone's friend is everyone's lackey.

147. You remain receptive, open to others, without loosing your your own interests ; that's what you tell your fellow man.

148. You don't have to apologize for any other occasion, unless it's a necessity.

149. A tree that knows to bend will not be broken by the wind.

150. We want to highlight the dangers of this development.

151. Social talks are based on equations.

152. If one is faced with direct talks or evidence, one

can directly answer with:

When?

Who?

Why?

Ask questions to see if the person concerned is in doubt.

153. Taking the whole situation into consideration, comparingthe opportunities, there would be no support for him. That's why I have taken the decision not to proceed. It would be flogging a dead horse. That comparison is a bit irreverent, but the case is clear.

Note

_____

_____

_____

_____

_____

_____

154. I give you this as added information, not as an excuse.

155. I don't sit on the same level as you are, therefore I cannot go on with you.

156. A little mucus seems to me more appropriate than threatening with a Court case.

157. If you cooperate with a tort you will have with no doubts limited rights.

158. If one is experiencing something, one searches for security at fellow sufferers.

159. Responsibility is not only to your environment, people, family, but also to yourself. Make sure you do not undermineyour own position. You will then be a clown.

160. That stems from frustration.

161. It is brain work, you can't excelerate that.

162. Sometimes you need to look at how it works, what works, rather than how it should be, what it should be.

163. What do you hope? Hope comes from the despair. You should cherish hope. Sometimes against the dismal odds.

164. I do not want a showdown. I don't want to argue with you as an authority.

165. Could you explain to me the actual legal bases on which you that think it can come true?

166. In case of questions or the service could not be better, or the accounting could not be better, etc. Through this kind of questions it shows that it's not good enough. On the way we can make improvements is under discussion now.

167. A man with a right or left philosophical belief.

168. That is sentimental error and as result a big one.

Note

_____

_____

_____

_____

_____

_____

169. It is better to have less well in your familiar environment than to go on adventures in foreign lands.

170. Who has the power, must be humble.

172. The situation has a stormy development recent days.

172. Revenge, even if is that sweet, is not acting with common sense.

173. There is already a formula for solving the problem, but apparently there is very little progress.

174. In a discussion to strengthen your position, you can say: "I don't want to have the last word, but the core issues, that's what it's about."

175 The result does not meet the expectations.

176. As true as I stand here, I'll submit a protest letter.

177. Party interest takes precedence over loyalty to a person.

178. That reasoning comes from the left wing or liberal wing.

179. For example: there must be a solid and democratic alternative visible.

180. That leads to an inexhaustible source of legitimate protests.

181. In some cases it is necessary to sacrifice a lot in order to preserve everything.

182. Someone on the dock.

183. Do you think that he will grant your request?
"If it is up to me sure."

184. It is better that one envies you your luck, then complain about your adversity.

185. You'll be in a deep darkness of trouble if you're not careful.

Note

_____

_____

_____

_____

_____

_____

186. How do you solve that problem? I wonder how.

187. In case of damage: "In comparison with what I could be that not enough."

188. Some objections are wellfounded, another unfounded, but those are for improvement.

189 At criticism "Oh well, fun is different, but it does show that our organization still is democratic and criticism is allowed. And there are you guys for"

190. In some circles the prevailing believers are paternalistic what means: "keep them ignorant and dependent"

191. Initially it was said to me that I was an outsider, had no experience. I have learned quickly.It is also a comment on all subjects against newcomers. If it was the ever lasting thuth there would be never,new young lawyers, notaries, teachers, bank employees or bakers.

192. I have taken note of your point of view.
I do not agree with your point of view.

193. How can one resume communication:

1. "Is there anything else you would like to say?" If no: Well, then, I would like to make a comment.

2. I see that it's difficult to talk for you. Maybe there is something you can put difficult into words.

3. I don't know what made you stop with that. I wonder if this is related to what I said.

4. The previous time a silence fell, you said that it had to do with what I had said, had done, or with your experience. Can you tell me more about it?

194. The other party declares that they are still the representative, or still want to talk."We have told the other party that his attitude during that (.......................) has raised many questions and by this his credibility has been affected. "

195. Borrowing costs, budgetary always more than save. You must only have to a sacrifice in advance

196. Advantage of voluntary work is the added value where the Government can't meet.

Note

_____

_____

_____

_____

_____

_____

197. The latecomer by his performance seems to say: "my time is more important than yours, therefore you can wait until I amfinished."

198. He is accused of that.. offence. What I hear let so many possibilities open from serious involvement to total innocence.

199. He had every confidence that the Commission, the Court or his employer would be swayed

200. It is very important that people should know where they stand. The decision making process should be transparent. If decision making is incalculable, this has a crippling effect on the people, especially if they are accustomed to clarity and responsibility. Everything can then stagnate. It works highly demoralising on the organization , the morale drops. Innovation and entrepreneurship are coming under pressure.

201.. Why should I know better?

202. If I want to communicate with the others, seems to me the most appropriate way to do that directly and not through you.

203. You talk about a storm in a teacup. The investigation will prove that I have told the truth; and facts don't lie. I'm not worried.

204. In love and war is not everything goes according to the rules.

205. I hope this action, this request is not lost and that it willachieve its goal and will reach the receivers, attendees.

206. An essential part of our democratic system is the right of self-determination of each member of the community, at least to the extent that the rights of fellow citizens do limit it. The principle of equality is very important. Equal cases to be treated equal. Unequal unequally

207. If someone says, invoking your feeling. "Do you trust me?" Then you can safely say: "Have you done something causing me not to trust you?"

208.. Why should I know better?

Note

209. If someone sends you a question about a confidential issue, can you say: "That's a question for you but the answer in mine."

210. If you do not want to give the purchase price of something for whatever reason say that is was a bargain.

211. With aggressive questions or objections, ask a quiet why question.

212. If there are to many questions can you say: "I don't need to answer all your questions."

213. If someone keeps asking your opinion to say: "You need to stop getting my opinion, I hope you feel that too."

214. In the case of unexpected questions can you say: "I do not like sneaky questions, please no other question?"

215. If you want to do a proposal , say: "I want to ask you a question to see if you can reach your goals in a constructive manner. Is that good for you? "

216. You will receive a proposal to be involved in something then you can say: "Can I think about it a few days and come with some ideas on how I can help?"

217. In the case of delicate issues one can reply: "We must also be prepared to review this issue from a more psychological side and a creative solution where both parties are happy with."

218. Watch that fair comparisons are made wherever it appears, and if possible, do not apply comparisons. Say: "Let's leave it in my case."

219. That's theoretical. I don't think it will be so

220. When you took office there were many promises, but now it appears to be different; How comes that? It is clear that at the time we were overly optimistic.

221. I don't know how his thought process, but he has a signal.

222. That's theoretical. I don't think it's that.

Note

_____

_____

_____

_____

_____

_____

223. People who make something clear sound hard for us. While they are not at all hard.

224. I am, either directly or indirectly, or tacitly involved.

225. How do you rate it? "I'm not the conscience of the people."

226. If you don't know the answer just say so. Man cannot know everything.

227. I don't hold them on other people's actions.

228. How do you rate it? "I'm not the conscience of the people."

229. we will that change? "That's an idea."

230. He's got a lot of criticism; What do you think of that? Criticism of him partially I agree. But I would use other words.

231. Even though I do that I'll keep the one I am. I want life to be more pleasant.

232. I enter everything that is intelligent. That idea of yours draws me not at all, but there are interesting aspects.

233. In a slip, one can say I will review the situation

234. Your own wallet is despite all nice thoughts, still the only by which you must pay.

235. I don't have any frictions with anyone. I only want my rights.

236. This is a hypothetical question and I would ask you the same; that I do not go on in.

237. That's what you are saying is inappropriate.

238. Do you feel misunderstood?
"No, but I also felt not overvalued."

Note

_____

_____

_____

_____

_____

_____

239. I'm not people shy, but I do not like to step off on people.

240. That's at least a little lucky situation.

241. That is a (bad) example of what can happen if not careful

242. I am not Hitchkok?
"That wouldn't be a bad example."

243. Don't you think that as a result, frictions arise?
"Is is possible. But that's a challenge for us. "

244. How did that happen?
There are different theories about. I don't know.

245. Working with him has an advantage, that I don't have to work with you.

246. What people know about themselves, which makes them afraid.

248. In the case of persistent accusations you can say: "if someone told you those things about me to you, you are brainwashed."

249. He has abandoned you?
"No, he has retreated to think."

250. The limits of the permissible.

251. Sometimes one must be content with insufficient information about the actual state.

252. Some individuals live in the assumption, have the illusion that they enjoy high regard.

253. What happens if you do not agree with each other?
"In that case we will help each other where we can."

254. Understanding is anything other than agree.

255. Look you must make no comparisons, but consider the situations on a case-by-case base.

Let's leave it at my case.

256. Deliberate concealment of facts (cheats) is very
different from the not fully reveal what you think at some
point.

257 If, for example, your adviser comes and says: "if he
gets the majority I will draw back, in that case you must do
it yourself." Depending on the situation this may have two
sides. Or he is no longer able to guard your interests or he
has other interests and puts you under pressure (blackmail).

258. Do you think that is acting with common sense?
You will find that good?

You say: "I appreciate your concern for common sense."
"I appreciate your concern for the well."

259. By saying that this is your final offer is you can come
back to it later with the statement: "it was not my very last
bid."

Note

_____

_____

_____

_____

_____

_____

260. In the case of errors or harassment, etc. you can reply with:

"that's sloppy and in social or other way can not be tolerated."

261. In times of adversity is the ingenuity of people much bigger than in times of prosperity.

262. In the event of a problem you can lay everything out and ask: what can you do for me?

263. If employees of a company do not have the right attitude and there is a lack of information, that may have consequences for the turnover.

This includes:

- correctness

- manners

- service

Service means no drudgery

264. As a surrogate for internal problems will people choose external threats.

265. We are with two or three parties here, if you want we can all go wrong. So let us work together.

266.. In some comments can you say: "You say so,that means that you have a lot of experience with that."

267.. If you want to interrupt someone you can say: "I was justwondering what you were going to say, when you started talking. Would you say it again? "

Note

_____

_____

_____

_____

_____

_____

Note

_____

_____

_____

_____

_____

_____

Note

Note

_____

_____

_____

_____

_____

_____

Note

_____

_____

_____

_____

_____

_____

265 Inspirational Quotes

Motivational Quotes

and

Positive Quotes about Life

With these quotes you will always have an answer for your questions. You will be able to manage your conversation very well.

Procrastination

The major reason why you may fail is procrastination. Procrastination is the regular delaying of your duties and activities for a long time. When you are procrastinating you simply refuse to pick up a tool and start working. In such case it does not matter how important the work is. You are not concerned about the consequences that may follow from further delaying your duty. Do not let this happen to you.

www.ingramcontent.com/pod-product-compliance
Lightning Source LLC
Chambersburg PA
CBHW060417190526
45169CB00002B/942